Patriarchal Advisory!
This book contains explicit
abuse of interpunctuation.

And I didn't even bother to get the label design rip-off accordingly outlined.

2

One-Hitting the Wonders

Kristian Carlsson

The Controversy

This page is all faded.
It is page 4.
It is a copyright page.
This page comes with complimentary WiFi.
It is the webpage of the unabridged chapterlessness of this fluent version with puppeteers.
It is chapter one with one as a split second of Air Force One.
This page is your White House and still it becomes more.
This page is here to let your bacon drip.
This is the page where the book drops its trousers.

— *Word play in all seen, noise in no scene.*

6

Disclaimer

No fictional language has been harmed in the nonfiction portions of this piece of literary work.

8

Proclaimer

The book portion of this book is already up and running. This might be highly irregular according to the end of this book.

Geography

You are here:
ISBN 978-91-87341-08-3

You are here:
Page 10

You are here:
:)

And here you are:
!

The Square

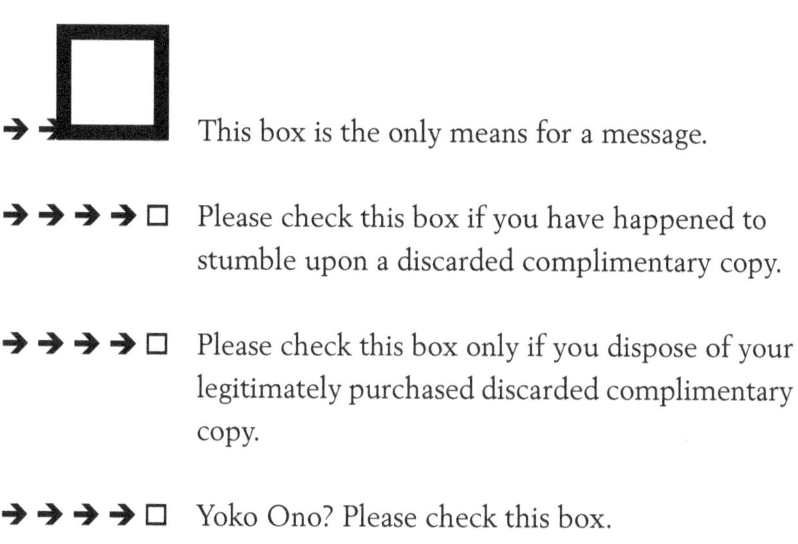

➜ ➜ This box is the only means for a message.

➜ ➜ ➜ ➜ ☐ Please check this box if you have happened to stumble upon a discarded complimentary copy.

➜ ➜ ➜ ➜ ☐ Please check this box only if you dispose of your legitimately purchased discarded complimentary copy.

➜ ➜ ➜ ➜ ☐ Yoko Ono? Please check this box.

¶

This text should appear
normal. If it doesn't, start
over at the top of this page.

Pay-Per-View

Nothing new at the World's Fair of Interpunctuations:
Souvenirs… Novelties… Party tricks…

The Tract

Interpunctuation is the circumstantial evidence of linguistics.

The clouded judgement of a comma is a misdemeanor.

Singing is language body building.

Allegiance Poem

I swear

By ¬,¬ [the double hyphenated comma]

u+S+a=$

≠ ABC; [abc raised to the power of semi colon]

Brute Treble Dice Poem

Modern Wonders

The déjà vu of a déjà vu.

The lifetime of a chance.

The illusion of the non-illusive.

Life is more obvious than time.

The post-mortem déjà vu.

Theme Parks

Theme park of obvious lies.

Theme park where the obvious lie.

Theme park of déjà vu.

Theme park of theme parks.

Theme park of divorces.

The Mind Games

I wear a wig on my mind.

You're always off my mind.

My mind is full of mines.

My mind is bullet proof.

Snow White & the 7 Dwarfs

I'd 8 them.

The Kiss & Make Up Widescreen Poem

(At Nine Frames Per Eternity)

)   (
)   (

)   (
)   (

)   (
)   (

)(
)(

Outlived

I've proved fit to survive Hollywood endings of the 20th century.

At the Oh

Oh, indeed!—as it seems.

Oh dear!, it's an *Oh no!*, for sure, as far as I can hear.

Oh to the letter.

Oh I pity thy Oh.

Short-Listed

Face food. Brain food. Finger food. Food fist.

Quizzed by the test of time.

Announcements

We're having the twins of a lifetime.

I'm declining birth-rate.

Their narrating congruity
    is by approximation.

¶

This t?xt shouſd appea☐
nor·mal. If it doesn't, start
over at the top of this page.

The Promise I

Soon the flipside of this page can be your pet.

The Promise II

Now the flipside of the previous page can be your pet.

In Trivia

Trivial detail: Trivial detail.

The trivial round: Circle.

Trivial circumstances: Circumstantiated circumcision.

Trivial gift: A pair of umbrellas.

Trivial joke: Giveaway rain.

A Rhetorical Pause Anti-Poem

Shit, I forgot to dedicate this piece of shit
to anybody,
is there anybody out there?

Some make-believe president PEZ secretary shat on the chat
online through the WiFi of a previous page
to cover up the Edward Snowden dedication,
the Pussy Riot dedication.

Please recapture the digital files here (in invisible ink or the jam of the 1987 Spaceballs movie or the pumped up Jam of Technotronic in 1989): _______________________________

____

____

____

____

____

____

____

____

____

____;

or make some origami folds to make a Memory stick or a video capture card out of this page.

Oh shit, this is section 3 and the pause has now become a beautiful centerpiece, give it a centripetal spin and it will tear the anti-revolutionary spinsters apart.

Read this period as the center of the book:

●

(4)   ⤢

                                                    ⇨ ⇨ ⇨ ⇨
Here is the beginning of an emptied room.   ⤢
In which you can legally have an abortion. Please use the
sterilized semi colon attached, to make this your own life.

☐   Bye-bye fetus—for this time—till another time, hook up
the umbilical cord to this colon:

                                                    :

☐   Bye-bye pre-baby—for this time—till the next time,
breast- feed on this comma:

                                        ,

☐   Raincheck.

The PEZ Dispensers

Alas, a Semi Colon PEZ.

Alas, the Capital I PEZ.

Alas, the Condom PEZ.

Alas, the Each Alas PEZ.

Anima

1.

tin zax zap
bah vai ben
fin kin ace
tow ski fee
use tee gum

2.

Any mole.
Anemia awe.
An eye mall.

To the Letter

I will try to translate this. Axis of a Will.
A wack.
Iron.
No core era.

Fuck Off Sonnet (The Whatever Poem)

((Participate to use only in rage)) (((Warning: Never fill in the blanks unfulfilling all the lines))) (((This is a "this-is-not-a-joke-poem-to-be-taken-seriously-and-kept-at-nightstand-as-a-loaded- gun-only-sonnet"))) ((((When in use with Shakespearean rhyme schedule this poem is lethal as a jackhammer)))) (((((When in use with Italian rhyme schedule this poem is lethal as a jack-knife.)))))
((((((This poem might become RAMBO[ROCKY])))))))
([7]In shorthand this sonnet is entitled "Not untitled")[7]:

Exile Conjugation

I ran
You ran
They ran
Teheran

The Mugshot

Semi-colon was my first beard in profile.

The Proverbs

!. You're old enough to be your own father.

!. It's no picnic. It's a piece of cake.

!. No bag suits my case.

!. Breed between the lines.

A Shot at Tales

1. Once upon a time-out.

1. Once upon Times Square.

1. Once up on time schedule.

1. One soup on time. One's pup in prime.

1. Once upon an "oh!"

Semi Short Stories

A.K.A. To make a long story short would make the short story too long.

y. He only meant trouble by the dry cough from always getting his spit in the wrong throat.

y. The unmasking was a limp by lame legs.

y. If only neither Marcia was to be neatly separated from the brand-new scatter.

y. Evil eye for eye-candy. Stubborn Santa.

Moreover One-Lined

Marx Twain

The Adventures of Lev Trotsky

Ice Axe Press

movue adaptuob (A.K.A. movie adaption)

with Che as T.

More-Ever

I'd hate to see you continue reading (me) now.

Has the previous screening in your cinematic brain already ended?

Here's the remake
in an unabridged adaptation by the punctuation marx.

Brain Poems

I.

The brain is a sponge-bath to the skull.

II.

Your skull would be braces to my milk toothy brain.

III.

Your brain is the charm bracelet of my brain.

¶

This t?xt should appeal
nor·mal. If it does, start over

¶

This text shouldn't appear
normal. If it does, start over
at the top of this page.

The Sellout

Dreams of cranes.
It's a piss of cake.
Cream to drain.

The Funnel

No, it was a cone. Turn
the page upside down for
the funnel to function properly.

The Apple

Not only because I say it *is* an apple. The letters are an apple to the point. The period is an apple to the saber-toothed cat of a jawesque comma.

ᴂ

? and ¶
are the hammer and sickle of the letters

no line brake when a question is raised
or else
oh
too late
report to the penance service on the double

straighten your questionability
chisel the jaw line of your sentence with a ";"

go fish Marx with a ":" on the ","

Spoiler Alert

The biopic of the hyphenation is X-rated for obvious reasons: The exclamation mark had to go nude on the dot for the leading role.

The Path

Trace the semi colon in real life
through the above mentioned text.

End (Entitled to Be Entitled)

a. (please use a permanent marker)

You have read: ____

By: ____

Copyright year (first edition): ________

ISBN: _______________________________

Publisher: _________________________________

____

b. (please use ~~semen~~ semi colon by proxy)

Mr/Mrs ______________________ (You) have reread (in
loud voice) the book: ____________________________
to (only one ";" mark, please): ☐ a relative   ☐ a relative
☐ a relative   ☐ a relative   ☐ a relative   ☐ a relative
☐ a relative   ☐ a relative   ☐ a relative   ☐ a relative
☐ a relative   ☐ a relative   ☐ a relative   ☐ a relative
☐ a relative   ☐ a relative   ☐ a president   ☐ a president
☐ a president   ☐ a president   ☐ a president   ☐ a president
☐ a president   ☐ a president   ☐ a president   ☐ a president
☐ a president   ☐ a fake president   ☐ a president
☐ a president   ☐ a president   ☐ a president   ☐ a president
☐ a president   ☐ other (where ";" is the only legitimate
character for spelling): ____________________

c. (Cross my heart and hope to die,)

☐   I solemnly declare this book to have ended here: x.

☐   I demand this book to be reprinted with the following page
count: _______ ; or the following page order: __, __, __, __, __, __,
__, __, __, __, __, __, __, __, __, __, __, __, __, __,
__, __, __, __, __, __, __, __, __, __, __, __, __, __,
__, __, __, __, __, __, __, __, __, __, __, __, __, __,
__, __, __, __, __, __, __, __, __, __.

I demand this book to be reprinted with the following page
cunt: ☐ ()   ☐ {}   ☐ ☐
             ☐ <>   ☐ []   ☐ %
             ☐ X   ☐ J   ☐ 0

Post-Preface

This text appears as normal:
This text appears as normal.

☐ Yes
☐ No
☐ It depends
☐ Kindly repeat the question as a proper question: "?"
☐ This text behaves as normal
☐ !

66

67

www.ingramcontent.com/pod-product-compliance
Lightning Source LLC
LaVergne TN
LVHW091527170726
843492LV00004B/1095